FIGURE IN THE DOOR

BY ARTHUR GREGOR

Figure in the Door   1968

Basic Movements   1966

Declensions of a Refrain   1957

Octavian Shooting Targets   1954

FIGURE
IN THE
DOOR

POEMS BY
ARTHUR GREGOR

1968
DOUBLEDAY & COMPANY, INC., GARDEN CITY, NEW YORK

"When water is realized, wave and sea vanish."

Sri Atmananda

CONTENTS

I

The Likeness 3
The Calm 5
Cypresses 7
What Is Human in Me 11
Reply to a Friend in New England 13
Shadowplay 15
Estufa Fria 17
The Love-Fanatic 20
September Song 22
Don Carlos, Saturday Afternoon 24
Exiled 25
Snow on This Deserted Street 26
Autumn Mood 27
The Minor Key 28
Landscapes of the Soul 30
You Were There 33

II

The Old Canal at New Hope, Penna. 37
Dreams 39
First Snow, Brooklyn Harbor 41
Awakening Mystery 46
Late Last Night 48
Schwanengesang 49

III

Irreconcilables 55
Unencumbered 57
What Gift Is This 58
Enchanted Flowers 60

IV

Wandlung   67
Poem   69
Some Elements of Drama   70
Lines on the Departure of a Friend   72
I Dreamt There Was a Knock on My Door   74
The Diplomat   75
Lament for a Gifted Man   76
The Non-Heroes   77
Sa Riera   79
Encounter at Tehuixtla   81
Past Dusk   85
The Mist from Tree to Tree   86
Requiem   87

V

Gentle Lamb   93
Afterthought   95
More on the Theme of the Stranger   96
Innkeeper's Wife to Itinerant Stranger   97
Said in Confidence   98
Today's Troubadours   99
Concerto for Diverse Instruments   100

VI

A High Estate   105

VII

To a Young Poet   115
The Unworldliness That He Creates   119
Short Poem   129

— I —

THE LIKENESS

How can you live, how exist
without assurance of
or at least the memory of
someone, something
fantastic, marvelous
always behind you,
a hand, grip on your shoulder,
a presence surrounding you
as a shell surrounds what lives inside?
Song closer to you than flutter to wing!
Word more antique than age!

Without it—call it intimacy,
your intimate connection—
how do you stand vis-à-vis
the multiplicity of things,
a tree, fence, grass, person in your path?
Unless you find in them
that quality no one defines,
how do you love, what do you
whisper, what song
do you share in the dark?

Without it I am as someone
lost from his caravan
a sandstorm whipping him;
someone out to find help on a frozen sea,
man alone on a waste of ice
imagining as the vast and hazy

emptiness absorbs him
a tattered though victorious
humanity coming toward him,
soldiers linking arms,
a populace with banners
singing and beating drums.

Without it
I am cut off.
I await its sound.
I ravage memory
for sight of it, its melody.
I shape with bare
and desperate hands
its likeness in myself.

THE CALM

1

Attempt at all times closeness to
the conflict you are in.
Not so as to dwell upon
dulling details of the cause
but to be aware of this:
that you are always in between
a white-clad calm that
at long intervals comes down
and the steady turmoil at the base:
a sea seething,
a field devastated,
a man weeping, stone and dust
turned human for as long as
being human can be endured.

2

Closeness to the conflict is
your nearness to its source.
The more fully a singer sings of
the pure anguish of your state,
the deeper the thought in you
that you too are being heard.
The turmoil in the water is often in
the surface that is thin.
When you cry because where you had been
the coast was calm, your small boat

in the sand left upside down,
the white-clad figure moving toward you
spanning sea and sun,
bemoan, bemoan it is no longer so!
The calm that will come again
was long ago!

CYPRESSES

1

A row of cypresses young and frail
on a Tuscan hill.
Gentle as a group of brides
they rise from a firm base,
from a deep green
to light blue space
that will not be theirs—
conflict to which they
as other slender
growing things are heirs—
keeping intact
a complex dark inside,
a leafy cave where bats hide
and winds add
sound to the secret
growing things inherit.

2

Nobly they grow
as if they understood
the meaning of growth,
the true meaning of growth.
They grow from a green so deep, so dark
the eye cannot tell the shades apart,
to a blue so fine, so thin,
its calm finds

correspondence in the heart.
And in between the two extremes
they form a darkness to contain
things that light can blind
and human happenings that—
though they must be—
should be kept
from being seen.

3

Sheep come up
to run between and rub
their fur against the trees.
When they do this
things hidden there
fly out although the light
will aid them not,
and others who had hoped
to be unobserved
and not noticing by whom
they were disturbed
run out across the grass.
The shepherd holds
a cornflower between his teeth
and pulls his hat's shadow
down his face.

4

When a storm drives by,
firm at the root
they bend at the top,
bend as though they were brides
lowering their heads

at the moment when
a force they do not understand
overcomes them
and something is being said
that has the sound of bells,
and something is being signed,
and something is being sung
that has in it the sound
a wind might weave with leaves
inside the darkness of trees.

5

Cypresses slender and young
on a hill in Tuscany.
Fully grown
they will be slender still,
will give to the scene
a solemn line,
solemn as thin smoke
rising up into a cloud.
Old, beautiful growth
that on a gentle hill arose,
that held within its leaves
whispers that have turned to grief,
flutterings that have long been stilled,
timid, flying, running things
that have rotted on the ground.

POSTSCRIPT

Cypresses are taller than most trees.
Space shows no mark of strain or tear
due to their stately rise,
due to their heavy fall at death.

[9]

To the ancients the cypress was
a proper symbol of the dead
sacred to Pluto of the underworld.
Probably because this tree
ennobles the countryside,
its foliage turns black in time,
space is indifferent to its death;
or because, popular as
material for musical instruments,
the wood of the cypress has
the properties that art demands.

WHAT IS HUMAN IN ME

What is human in me—
dreams that repeat,
incitement of figures
riding in on waves—
sorrow in me
that what arises
must in like manner fade—
face bent over my sleep
easing the pain when I woke—
what is meaningful to me
must from time to time at least
be my reality,
not unlike the soil
a plant needs to grow,
must be around me—
faces in whom
is deeply inscribed
feeling for suffering,
eyes that state
facts that can't be said.
No one can take bloom in hands,
though it may seep through pores
and make one shudder in the dark.
Walls I seek
with flowers strung from top,
the height where hidden gardens start,
full life of the senses, of the heart,
floats I can imagine but not see—

the invisible suggested by
the visible to stir
what is human in me.

REPLY TO A FRIEND IN NEW ENGLAND

I have your note.
Sorry to read you're lonely.
You have not found the joy you went for.
I know the bay you're visiting.
There the visual things
suggest the condition you feel,
flap in one's soul
like laundry hung to dry.
The sky is static there,
thin clouds the color of
swans' wings let through
a light that reaches corners
but has not the power
to illuminate.

Water beats against the stones
below the strip where people sit,
the boats out in the bay
look as though they give themselves
to being tossed about,
and not much happens.
The shadow of a bird
(wings spread fully out
the bird seems not to move,
seems painted on the air)
hovers over the reflection in
the water of a boat,
gray spreading over gray.
Shadows in this bay

that seek each other out,
cannot be kept apart,
nor does one blank the other out
escaping thus the separateness
that all decry, the flow
and sway of each with which
each must identify.
Is this then the law
that all must learn to live
who visit where you are
or any other strip of coast:
identity must be retained?
loneliness is part
of being self-contained?

In this bay where you have come,
where the coast is defined
by what you see—
by monotone and static sky—
you like others must confront:
the limited return
of what you want.
All day long the light is faint.
The repeated view of sails,
taken for white flags
implying hope, is bleak.
You have not found another way,
no other way but inward for
the self-assuring joy you seek.

SHADOWPLAY

Dead to the world, I was cast back
to move again among familiar shapes.
The state where I had been
cannot be described. There were
no objects there, but in
full strength and in pure form
the presence that takes speech
and mind away when feelings
are stirred by a person's momentary stay
pale as early evening in the door.

I knew when I was back it was
not nothingness had held me there.
That part in me which bears
no semblance to my body's line
on paper or in falling light
was then about to be received
like a cloth brought to be laid
across arms wide as space,
by a love gentler than air
and voices, voices behind clouds.

Not yet allowed, some forces dark
and fleeting came and drew me back—
from high walks where structures hold
all time and things that pass—
back to shadows that glide across
the shadow of my hands,
back to the movement of clouds,

the light at dark, the noted hush,
the moment of the figure in the door,
back to my repeated effort among
the things where I have walked before.

ESTUFA FRIA*

1

Clouds the shape of
chalk tracings of wings
above the city by the sea.
The shutters closed at noon.
A wave rippling far out.
A murmur running down
an empty street.
Around the winged statue in
the port people sit,
cars are parked.

The hand of the giant clock
has turned one slot
to the sound of bells.

Movement starts.
Wave and wing begin to pale.
An air drifts by
as if from foreign parts.

In an area set aside
for music, birds and solitude,
book-in-hand a figure walks.

* A tropical garden in Lisbon.

2

Dissolve, body, forget
the melancholy of
solitary steps.
Be leaf of palm,
be glitter of small birds.
Be tiny pool,
the glidings of
the single swan.
Music pours from
all sides, a silence
from the wings above.
And what the book contains
is nothing but the spelling of

one word
one word . . .

3

. . . body of love

even the faded figures
in ruined frescoes,
in restored rooms
the portraits by famous masters
fix their eyes on you

the singer's hand
points at you

cloud wings and murmurs
hang about your head,
a diffuse succession
from the sky

and far above the historic plains,
the mountains far away—
whirls of snow
like a dreamer's gestures in the air—
lift up and stream to you

body of love
by the sea.

THE LOVE-FANATIC

The dilemma of wanting not just
to taste but to possess
glorious, impossible love
can be described as this:
I have dared alone in my boat
far out beyond where any sea-
searching fanatic should.
I find the shape I want to hold.
We burn in a burning haze.
Incited by this fire
and again seeking out the spot,
the shape on water cannot be found.
Though spirit hungers, I share
the urge of hound for hound.
I hear in the winds nothing but
chords from lost love's lyre
and a turbulent bloodstream
makes me seek far and farther out.

No flares or warning signals
are sent aloft from shore.
Indifferent to my spirit's needs
life goes on there as before.
True, special gardens are there
for healing, serene and secure.
But it is not serenity I've dared
far out for, but love
for which there is no cure.
For which I've set sail again

seeing in my mind a priest
with crucifix above the sea
to pacify this storm or bless
the drowned who had to learn that
the vision on the water—
not merely an angelic creature
but fiery, perfect flesh and blood—
is a reality
they could not keep, but found.

SEPTEMBER SONG

A cool evening in early fall.
The evening brisk yet frail
thin as a river's skin,
like a canvas of air open to tracings:
people, shops, traffic lights and cars
briefly imprinted on the evening's surface—
a painter's strokes on a watery base.

On the radio a rarely performed
Schubert work. Vienna a long time ago.
I walked there once. Ah, much more
than once. A statue in
a basin in a square dedicated to
the penniless, the dreamridden
genius, Schubertplatz, Schubert-
gasse, Schubertallee—

a damp evening, the streets
lit dimly by electric bulbs
in streetlamps where not long ago
gas had flickered,
the whole flickering evening drifting by
in the darkness under the bridges
of the Danube canal.

Adagio. The width, the height,
the length of the evening spread,
have far-reaching effects
like a crack in a glass,

the brush of time on a sensitive brow,
a pebble on a surface that cannot endure.

Adagio. The slowness, transitions
from hardly discernible shadings
to deepening frown, the pain
that comes with the changes in music,
creeps into one's being like the breath
from gratings in streets
when the temperature has fallen to zero,

these have not the power now
to rouse a question.
The question is gone.
Gone also the youthful agitation
that there is one.

In supreme naturalness
fades the statue of Schubert's
nineteenth-century head.

In supreme naturalness
the shifts and fadings
of a brief walk one brief evening
one brief evening one brief fall.

DON CARLOS, SATURDAY AFTERNOON

Alone! Who does not know the meaning of
alone? Granted, there is a world outside,
houses and streets are wet,
people run in and out of cars.
In the story sung on the air
each character is in the end alone.
A Spanish prince still loves the woman
who has become his father's bride.
A conquering Court attends the saving
of fallen Christians at the stake.
Although one hears a lofty gloria,
the prince in prison chains cries out,
betrayed, he thinks, by the one he loved
and by the friend in whom he believed.

Does it really help that being alone
is one condition shared by all?
The drama off-stage is no less complex.
Although one may assume that
disparate parts that do not always lock
in place are woven by a common thread,
the burden is not lessened for all that.
Not lessened by bewildered heads
and muffled cries, nor by the fact
that the sky's been agitated all day long,
that men in raincoats stumble across
slippery roofs, and that the very air
is dense with wriggling bacteria
which show up under a powerful glass.

EXILED

Where will you go? Where now the rooms
once kept ready for you, the old
couple on hand to welcome you,
the garden just as it was when last
you visited, just as it was
as far back as you remember it—
golden the landscape when you stood there
late in the afternoon?

Where is it now, that place where you
belonged so naturally, the formal
growths, the house, the sunset-sights,
the dark turns of corridors—all these
as much alive in you then as they
were real once, summer after summer
in the country not far from town?
Now they are gone. Thoughts of them

stay on like tatters of a sail.
Memory will pale, and you have no
way now to turn and walk into
the interior you knew so well.
Another storm, one final gust,
your tattered thoughts will be as dust.
To keep alive the glow within
of what was once your ground, your home,
you need the plot, the trees, the stone.

SNOW ON THIS DESERTED STREET

Snow on this deserted street
who caught your gleam,
the fire and the frost,
your origin
lost now in the unintended look
of few inhabitants
who cross the street at extreme ends
and do not meet?

Snow, your fiery innocence
need not endure
small thoughts of those
who stop perhaps to cross
who do not stop to meet
through you their own whiteness
sole and unsoiled
in a deserted street.

You are the sign from which
all run. Whiteness on a street—
left bare, withdrawn—
so like the body and its sheet
before the waking starts
and cleaners seize your glow.
Before they come, you are!
O snow! Pure snow.

AUTUMN MOOD

The smell that flames impart to air
of a fire tended and controlled
in a garden or clearing in
an autumn wood

stirs the recumbent fellow in
the body's inner room
where not a hallway leads,
no easy turn of knob can reach.

Pensive and full
of weeping thoughts he lies,
to a violent strength aroused
when invading smells and sounds proclaim
the burning season dies.

THE MINOR KEY

It is the minor key I crave,
full absorption in it,
view of a Spanish bay,
a single sail where cliffs
jutting out form a kind of gate,
perfect the sea and sky beyond;
the music in a Renaissance court,
idealized love turned
to pure lament on lutes
and viols; the grave walk
of figures garbed as though
statues in Roman times;
the doves in frescoes,
the eyes of supplicants,
and so much more of like intent.

To live the conflict fully,
alike for many a creature:
the lower half held back
by the weight of place
and pulls for which
there is no obvious evidence—
underwood, desires gone wrong,
a taste for the world's rewards—
the upper parts seeking
contact with that of which
early representations tell,
the unimagined wonder,
amazement in the voice,

the thin trail of birds
rising when bodies sleep.

This mode of strain I crave,
full concert of the pain
and anguish without which
the movement upward cannot be,
pray that its minor key
possess me with the force
natural to flowing things
streaming to their source.
And not allowed
nor ready to reside in
the realm toward which all flows—
its lasting splendors and
its spaciousness—crave
that I may lament with all I own
lack of its harmony where I am.

LANDSCAPES OF THE SOUL

1

Fragments flare up
fragments scattered across
landscapes of the soul.
Stone silences at high noon,
heads, poses whereon
light has thrown a cast
time cannot touch.

2

Many the movements of the men,
nomads taking with them
all they possess.
Many the tracks, the muffled intentions,
the massacred flowers
massacred soul-flowers in the snow.

3

A child I sang,
spun a fabric of life that is perfect,
of moments that would spew forth—
like petals from a fountain's mouth—
a love so great, so simple
death would dance, death
giving its whiteness to everything touched by its veils.

4

Attracted by the fragments,
by the promise they give off,
I stepped forth on the landscape,
I among men running in many directions,
men heaving boats,
men in carriages,
poor men singing love songs
with eyes closed.

5

The freshness that clung to my lids—
freshness accumulated in my dreams—
pure, pure, of unaccountable,
indiscernible, indescribable
and yet, uncontestable hue!

6

Men who pull boats down a canal,
men in carriages watching the landscape altering,

you who feel yourselves nailed to
the things you carry on your backs

you who have allowed yourselves to think
you're twirled by a power you can't escape:

hear, hear the melody
played on a single string.
Birds after birds rise from it.
Whiteness of veils.

Stand where you are. Incline your heads.
Let water accumulate!

7

Hale beyond stain,
magnificent however maimed,
whispers of a masterpiece:
are you not quite familiar with
suggestions of a flower
you have lived in dreams
and at least once, once at least
in this landscape,
this heart-rending tale?

8

A lily rests
a lily grows
secure in its roots
behind man's bones.

YOU WERE THERE

You were there. How else
could the scene have come
into its own, could ice
on the lake and that part
below the bridge that flows
and the trees   O bare wintertrees
their arms like a fork about
to dig hay from the sky,
have ascended like a soul?

And the birds! A vertical
one pecking on wood,
a sparrow perched on a log,
and the call like a bark
of a black one above,
each flutter, each sound
complete like a marvelous death,
and the reeds in a haze
of snow on the bank.

The palms of your hands
were in the trees where the birds
drove their beaks in the wood.
The fall below the bridge
streamed from the wound
in your side. And who was it
who else by your word
sang with each bird
and held on to a tree for support?

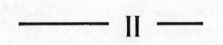

THE OLD CANAL AT NEW HOPE, PENNA.

It is not just a wish, this craving.
It is more as if one were demanding
the only thing to which one is
truly entitled: that which perhaps
one was, but yearns at any rate to be.
Surely, strong sensing such as this
must come from something that is.

Not a fact accomplished only by will.
Once this canal was busy. It is dead
now, although the waters still freeze.
This wish, true tradition assures us,
is acted out by whatever we do,
is a common, continued behavior
the dead are performing still:

That the heart may break; that in breaking
it may be remade, like rivers
that each had a special meaning
but which, at the place of meeting,
are rid of distinguishing marks:
rivers that once were shallow,
or known for the trade they carried.

In the same way, let the heart in breaking
become the heart of all.
Every stream, small
or widened into a river or fall,

flows down its path with rapidity
as if the current promised above all:
tall sprays, and generous space.

DREAMS

We have, most of us, had some indication
of a blissful existence in dreams
when our fathers, of whom we never expected
anything but the best when we were children,
appear before us with golden cloth over their shoulders
dressed for Holy Service, and waiting to be called
convey to us the simple grandeur
we once were certain would one day be theirs;
or when, in a shift of scene,
we come out on a far-off
though very familiar harbor,
watch boats glide in, magnificent boats
as we used to see on postcards when we were children,
liners crossing all oceans, and what moves us most
is when we behold how calm is the water
as if calmness and calmness alone
were the meaning of water rising
and falling away in perfect order,
washing up against the stairs
that lead to a court of worship, lead to
the city, and beyond the homes, mountains.
Do they not seem to suggest, these dreams,
they have been projected before us to serve us,
to give us to understand
a heightened sense of being exists
with which it is not only possible
but, since we have known it, imperative
to establish complete communion, strive for it,
or die? And that, having once succeeded,

a sense of superior well-being
such as might be experienced during a lifetime
of dedication to that which each calm
expression expresses, whose existence
can no longer be doubted, nor anything wished for
that is less than complete, will then be accomplished?
And revealing these heights to us,
do they not also tell us
that even the pain, our great pain
when we come back from them—dreams,
if dreams we must call them—to our daily
condition so out of proportion
with where we have been,
is in perfect order, as is the suffering
we try not to expose, to inflict it on others,
and the look of longing we cannot conceal?

FIRST SNOW, BROOKLYN HARBOR

1

Driven by a music of which their every move
in a mood of love, the loftier side of them
in dreams are parts; unconsciously out for a sign
that is a gesture of the song they do not hear;
who among those who stopped along the promenade
facing the waterfront could have regarded
the first flake of the first snow this season
as nothing but the substance that they are?

Unless someone had ventured out, had left
the customary ways of recognizing form
and light and shade; unless someone endowed
with a rare inner quality had looked
and found the single substance holding these
streaming from his eyes, breaking from the heart
where it lies and not unlike calm waters beneath
the frozen surfaces in mountain areas waits
beneath all icy grounds where light like sound
in the unsaid aspect in each song glistens
beyond sight;

                    unless someone had pierced
the surfaces and stood entirely immersed
within the substance of all forms, within
the very center of all thoughts and shapes
that like the very breath of time rise from
the one sure thing toward which all strive;

unless someone in such state had given
existence to the first flake falling and from
beyond the range of sight proclaimed the whiteness
that streaked across the eye in streams
and in a time too imminent to calculate
dissolved, absolved the heaviness of the world:

who among the solitary men looking out
beyond the river and the ocean piers
into a changed and changing distance, could
have known that these are closely linked:
the forms across the waterway, the lights
barely discernible that alternate, the snow
that falls, the physical significance of snow,
the revival in the hearts of solitary men
of dreams?

       How could they have known that these
are more than linked, are one with that
which glistens in and between the flakes,
are the same as what the fall of snow implies?

And what it evokes in them, how could they know
it is the same as what they—solitary men,
distances apart, gazing beyond the river,
ocean-landing where they stand—in this
first snow are looking toward, are looking at?

2

The thing itself that lives, the dominance
of that which is so close to all it is
the heart of all; in which the first sign
originates and descends into sight as snow,
whose nature is unfathomable although

in this and every scene implied by some
incomprehensible means like a music
that cannot be heard: O what they do not know
is that the distances expand within them:
what they are looking toward is where they are.

They do not know departure is the pain they carry;
that circumstance has forced on them a burden
the removal of which is the change they seek
in dreams of a journey and the joy they sense
of what it must be like the instant of arrival.

In a fall of snow, the first of the season,
they stand and dream and watch the footprints
disappear in the will of heaven; absorb the sounds
of water-objects drown in a deeper music,
and shiver as light breaks in their hearts
and something vastly woeful hangs at their eyes.

For, if these men are in no way exceptional,
if they are not endowed with a sacred privilege
to look and find the answer contained in the question,
fire in the ultimate regions of cold, arrival
in the act of departing, the indivisible total
in each divided vanishing footfall
as each flake contains all of the snow.
If it is not for them to set forth
provoking customary habits with
a selfless motive for daring and a song
to rely on from loss to finding, they cannot know this,
though they do surely sense how enormous are
the heights that exist within the pattern of Being:

Beyond their conditioned manner of reaching, near them,
with no more than a turn of their shoulder,

they can glimpse the regions of high-minded men:
the heart which is wisdom, the pleasure, the welcome,
the compassionate quality in music.
The burden circumstance has forced on them
is a condition abolished by a shift within them,
as the heaviness of the world is abolished by
a sudden decision which is the first snow
of the season.

*　*　*　*

And if they cannot know themselves
possessors of the single substance
of which all of the harbor before them,
and the forms that make up the harbor
and the transformation of everything in
and around them which they attribute to snow,
are made of;

and if they cannot assume the stand
that that which is in them, into which
each flake dissolves and all perceptions flow,
is changeless, and they the beholder of changes;—

they do, just the same, sense with longing
something of permanence, knowing, as they do,
only the changes; and for a moment absorbed
in a depth that is the quiet of the whiteness
descending, question:

what are they caught in?
Where does it come from, the dream, the thoughts
of which they are conscious? Has the snow
brought back the ways they knew as children,
dreams that have caused them embarrassment in gesture,
quick glances?

And if they cannot recognize
themselves in the radiance of unreal faces
like spirits in a net of snow; and if
what they know is not the supreme conquest
by achievement but the mystery like a sob
within them, they do, just the same, sense it:
the nearness that is far:

                    ranges of oceans,
distance and music in the sounds of water-objects;
and grieve for the breath of an angel they feel
in the footfall they cling to for an all-engrossing,
all-encompassing vastly beautiful moment
before the outlines that attest to the fact
that a human has been there, turn into snow.

AWAKENING MYSTERY

Leaving the place to which you are accustomed,
whose unknown corners sufficiently localized
you think of less and less
and forget them day by day;
leaving the place whose mystery
is never fully explored
because it has become familiar
and you do not accept
what you will never know,
that you will never know it
but forget that there is something hidden
behind your door,
something beyond the reach of lights
that you have missed, and do not know.

Leaving the place whose mystery is shrouded
because it has become familiar
and exploring the familiar is usually neglected,
it can happen one day
when you take a train out into the country,
that you find every road, every field,
every house and stream washed in a clarity,
each enriched by nothing but
its own quality:
color, shape, and angle of shade,
a horse grazing here, a bridge over there,
and something that is quick
in the distance, whose shape is lost
but whose shadow you see.

And when you pass by the brook
and behold the water in absolute stillness,
the backs of houses, a boat tied
to the bank, and you remark—
and it is only later that you know
you have remarked this—"How still,
how perfectly still it is,
the very black shadow of trees
in the water"; and directly thereafter think
of a woman weeping
because someone had made her understand,
and you are not sure if this was dreamt
or witnessed by you at some time, but know
that her experience at that moment
is something you now can comprehend,

and you are moved, so moved,
to have somehow been made to possess all this.
It is then, when peace and clarity
take hold of you and you are so at ease
you do not think to think:
then it might happen that you sense
the mystery you have not explored
in the place you left,
something hidden behind doors,
something beyond
the reach of lights that you have missed.

LATE LAST NIGHT

Late last night we drove through fog:
nothing but a vague onslaught at
the window: vapors, or was it breath?

the clouds of the earth coming at us
all along the road. In the watery
substance all turned the same:

lights around corners, dreams behind
rooms, the country wide as oceans,
the singleness in every name.

SCHWANENGESANG

1

Humble, in pose like the willow
at the water's edge, the willow
bending low; shy, unobtrusive;
in mist, or at the points in time
when extreme contrasts meet,
when merging cancels difference out,
hardly perceptibly there: a swan;

glides by in trembling elusiveness,
behind the screen of change—
an idea no one has ever seen—
to hearts straining for a silent
song is subtly evident
like the slightest wind
responded to by mostly little things:

leaves on the ground,
leaves of another season,
some tiny flies that lift
or crawl, a neglected bit
of paper note, a footprint
losing contour in the dust.

2

Nearby, another swan. The song
of the first rests on everything
surrounding him and is not heard,

but of the sound of the other
there can be no mistake:

It is the cry that gives
the unheard song its own
characteristic note, and draws
toward a common center those
that heed what it implies,

attracts such little things
that once were part of bloom,
of hope, of moving toward,
each once involved
in becoming whole and being real,
which was the state of each,
of which, in the case of man,
he is convinced without much thought,
until, torn, all turn obedient
in disguising nothing
in their much lesser form.

3

Two swans, one like the willow bent,
trembling for all this greater force,
the other's neck crying upward like a horn,
both equally entwined in mist,
each expressing differently
the one condition basic to them both:

each lives; each flames; each gesture dies
in an instant less than time;
their perfection, the total form of each,
caught only by the barest wind,
that air in which all die,

that air in which the pose of each
is transformed to accord
with standards of the invisible,
the changeless wing adorned
by all these changing things:
the swan's gesture; the swan's cry.

III

A GROUP IN MEMORY OF MY MOTHER

IRRECONCILABLES

How to explain that on the day
we knew disease had invaded her
who had brought us into the world,
that death had conquered her like a weapon
she would not escape for long,
the winter sun spread vastly
and with utter ease
giving sharpness to each thing,
making all things stand out
as usually they don't:
a line of ships rooted like rocks,
and people in the frozen streets
free and light as the breath
that clung to them like clouds.

Along the edge of the cold sky
a strip of deep lavender ran
like a streamer in a wind
pulled by an invisible string,

and the water in the port
made over by days of cold
looked chopped but permanent, as if
the sea were chunks of bottleglass.

And everywhere surfaces
giving off the winter sun
in a sort of game of catch,
throwing at each the light

that each received, so that
the effect was a jubilation,
a juggler's feat so fast,
so intricate a trick, the full
extent of its multifarious display
escaped our eyes. But the sense
that it was there, and that
it meant not to deceive
but to reveal a joy
did not elude us.

Yet we were driving to get to her
who we feared might soon be gone.
And how were we to reconcile
exuberance with what we were about?

That a car was taking us
to the condition we call death,
that extinction could occur
when the day showed itself
in a display so bright
it seemed a game of light,
that disappearance should
make sense when all about us
objects we could not name
flared up in a cold winter sun
and shone until we had to turn
from them as from a flame,
nothing in us could reconcile,
nothing in us could explain.

UNENCUMBERED

Almost a heap of bones
in your bed with iron guards
like rails around a grave,
what are you now to yourself?

All that you wove
as insects weave
nests like a net,
all that you cared about
of time within time,
child within child,

husband, father within man;
all that you strained for,
spun and spun, cut now,
cut now and gone
from your mind! Unencumbered,
mother
what do you find?

WHAT GIFT IS THIS

Mother, on your deathbed
it is we surrounding you—
who surrounded you when you
were well, each attending then
our separate ways which meant
for you distress at times,
at times your pride—
we who are wounded now,
the sign that you are acting out
our wound suggested on your brow.

What mystery is this
that with approaching death
and all the worst of miseries,
you are made to offer us
a gift, holding in
your trembling hands a bowl
toward which we fall
like bystanders on their knees
to bestow upon the ring
of rule and grace a kiss?

Though it is with loss we stand,
with lack of comprehension at
your bed, and are not comforted
by what is visible.
What gift is this?

You die and we lean forward
to let you pour on us
what you must pour,
we your guests and you our host.

ENCHANTED FLOWERS

1

She is a flower in the wind.
Her bloom is gone.
The wind must take her petals
one by one.
She brought joys to beholders,
stinging pain to intruders.
Lean stalk of a stem,
the wind once proud of her
now wails in and about her.
The seer cannot see herself.
Dying is the wind's full grief.

2

Flute, flute
be your utmost!
A column of thin smoke
in that forever distant distance of
perpetual light.
Thin shape by flowers
entwined as though by a snake,
the mood of dancers
collected in a heap.
Flute, flute
till I weep!

3

In total possession of themselves,
arrayed with every pollen, petal,
drinking insect each possessed;
arrived at their own enchantment,
arrived at last in that sphere
where storms do not enter,
where not they but the winds have died:
they hum to be thus collected,
humming absorb the anguish
of those about to cross over.

4

Flow gently, flower.
Children once again,
we weep at your going,
weep for a reception
adequate for one such as you,
absorber of light,
bearer of our misjudgment.
You who pity us when,
returned to our purity
for the instant of your going,
we cannot endure it
and you break out
in renewed petals
in the air above our heads.

5

Contained in the air
and spread across the distance

we take in in our days,
in the deep recesses of our beings
devoted to this enchantment,
striving to experience
flood of the scent
that pursues us: flowers
of numberless clouds, of wings
of wind falling toward each stem. . . .

6

You among the rare, the chosen ones
whose inner space is wind of scent,
do not insist on the attempt
to hold the bloom in trembling hands,
nor keep yourselves from trying.
To stand straight, in the distance your eyes,
alert in sleep, in all your worldly ways
to hints and nuances that seek
the fragrance that you are:
is there any more to do
to honor flowers praising you?

7

Who is alert is pious.
Imprints of things as they are
demolish notion and choice.
Who has the strength to replace
his will with the naturalness
of scented growth and death
touching body and eye,
glides across night and day,
is masterful, fragile as a bird:
exposed, exposed—alert!

8

In separateness, transition's bitter mark,
an admixture of the space that gathered them
and the touch of red, of green, of violet
upon the cloudlike paleness of the frost
that curls to kill beneath each stem:
so do all move across the plain
assigned to each for our days.
What has been said is said again.
Of shadowy substance is the dance.
What's concrete is beyond such circumstance.

9

In transition composed
the motion, pallor,
leaves of the rose.
In transition contained
the indwelling wind
that had languished once
on many a noble's parapet,
had lain within a flute,
had held upon a cheek
what to strong men is
a sign of the weak.

10

But no! They are fools
who see and say it so.
Grandest of all,
as experience second to none,
flowers that fall from eyes

as response to
a more than human,
more than time-conditioned
circumstance.
Petals that rain
when the wind must come
to shake at a stem.
Gently, flow gently then:
flower, breathless, human.

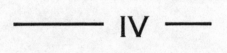

WANDLUNG

1

Day after day, comes fall,
sky and sea are gray.
Along the coast, beneath bare boughs
there is the threat of ice.
Seasons of blossoms
and of dying leaves
have tumbled down streams
seething at the estuary
free now of summer stars
and of discoloring shades.

It is a time brisk and stark,
devoid of former flourishes.
The last of the south-going birds
have flown past
on to their separate seas.
Only the shrill warnings,
the questioning blares
of northern birds
spatter the air.
A few late leaves drift by.

2

Down in the port
boats empty their registered cargo out
blurred in

the watery autumnal haze
as if the bales were ghosts.
Boat after boat
or so the dampened foghorns say.

3

Yearly, when summer's ease and fervor goes
young women mostly indoors,
young men in bars
have watery, melancholy eyes
that whisper of strangers
driving their horses up
uneven streets,
foreigners who whistle like winds
and sing.

Then will even the dogs lie low
so splendid, so rare—
and yet not surprising
almost in fact anticipated
as if expected year after year—
so commanding the sight
of the bright strangers
driving their black
wet horses
up the hill.

POEM

Along the edges of a tranquil sea,
along the line where a steep ascent
begins, a heron wades, then stands.
He is the only living thing about.
Silence shivers as if touched by sounds
subtle as the air that holds
the heron's spread blue wing.
He strains his neck, his mild hooks
barely in the sea, and lightly shakes
as if captured by another self
that glistened once like sun-held clouds
in regions where both sea and land
are shed. Where are these from,
vision and sounds subtle as the force
that set him down where sea recedes
and a steep slope ascends?

SOME ELEMENTS OF DRAMA

The scene: A Bathing Resort In Spain

A dark mist hangs upon the sea.
The change in sky is out of character,
and the weird behavior of the water.
Upset the summer guests walk up
and down as if expecting news.

Large birds not common in these parts
are perched on tops of cliffs
where on more ordinary days
the bathers sit to dry. To relieve
this mood, the owners of
hotels have put on jazz.

A table-umbrella torn from
its metal stand, turned inside-out
by an abnormal wind
lies unretrieved
like a disaster out of reach,
threateningly distorted
on a shunned, a battered beach.

What has happened?
What monster has broken forth
out of some dreadful mind
to pursue a ghastly need?
What ill-distorted shape
that stalks now on the sea,

hissing behind the air,
driving the waves, fist
upraised, clouding
the minds of men like mist?

No one can tell
the happening beneath
the fury and the lifting fronts
of sea, how long this turn
will last, and what
will be revealed

when the disturbance ends.
Silently the strange large birds
sit perched on cliffs.
Their seeing eyes are sealed.

LINES ON THE DEPARTURE OF
A FRIEND

When you wrote that you will leave, I said:
To sadness we will pay no heed.
Might as well stress each thing
that goes: the bluejay's call we heard
the while it snowed, the girl at the gate
who looked straight at us but turned
before we reached the road,
the music we were fondest of,
and other sounds and passing sights
of which nothing is left but thought.

Departure was of course part of
the meaning when you came.
Reading about one such as you,
imagining for long a presence which
would conquer death in one quick look
or move of hand, I thought myself
quite ready for the changes that ensue
when high purpose comes in your form
to sit before one like a faith.

Let all things come and go
should surely be the only attitude
toward that high visit briefly here,
the process by which are inscribed
events till they stay on. But now
you leave. Horns drone in
my mind. Your ship is gone.

I cannot shrug a gnawing sense
which makes me see a tearful face,
makes me bemoan a cause,
fix my mind on a date far hence
and on a foreign place.

I DREAMT THERE WAS A
KNOCK ON MY DOOR

I dreamt there was a knock on my door.
I opened. O power of the Real. Before
me stood a friend I had been told was dead.
"Come in. How glad I am," I said,

"Come in, come in, Ted." And off I ran
to tell the others he was here again;
to tell those in whom loss was deep, and pain:
the life of our friend was still the same.

How good to know there is no loss,
that life is beyond harm in those
who are humble before it, who honor it;
and this he sincerely and always did.

We were so glad we wept in gratitude,
not so much for what was restored as for that
which cannot be lost; and felt, for the sake
of what is real, death is a mistake.

And so, in a dream, shared the solace of
all-encompassing pure life and love.
Which turned to sorrow in the day.
For he is dead, and now lives on this way.

(in memory of Edgar Bogardus)

THE DIPLOMAT

Radiant as light in glass,
it must be knowledge of home
gives his eyes the look they have
always reminiscent of pure sight
as of a child just up and in
the frame of a window looking at
meadows, trees, a country road
streaked by a spring rain.

Such confidence must mean
home is not a distant land,
is imminent, a resting place
that does not let one down,
nor is it as a wooden wharf
tired fishermen step upon,
nor as a house a boy runs toward.

He is not a naïve emissary.
Carefully he speaks and to the point,
is at ease in the world
though reticent.
A true servant at his post
he knows well what must be
guarded and defended most,
which those he comes in contact with
soon realize,
so deep the calm in his eyes.

LAMENT FOR A GIFTED MAN

Whatever it was that gave
you radiant stillness like
a fluttering air, is gone.
You were the recipient once,
were the figure that seemed to walk
like someone wrapped in light
across an agitated bay or lake.
You could not accept
the apparition was
for our sake, not yours,
could not give yourself
to it enough to become
the radiance you were possessed of.
Now emptied of what
is so much bigger than you are,
you stumble on,
err, err,
a rower without oars,
and are off course
no matter where you are.

THE NON-HEROES

The story is not told of two young men
in ancient Greece, not friends or lovers
glorified for some heroic deed for which
they died placing gold-leaved wreaths
upon each other's brow; a fine spirit
with which their elders could identify.

These youths, and countless more,
were ardent friends because each was
possessed by a restless dream
to which they clung like erring children
in a forest to a distant gleam.
Spirited longing changed to horror
when one day each had to discover
the dream each thought the other had
was not the same, and thus betrayed—
though neither had intended it—
took to death in a scandalous way.

The dilemma abounds in modern times
though cowardice may be in evidence
where daring mattered once and pride.
A nameless yearning that pursues
the lives of wide-eyed, eager youths.
Unvoiced, with nothing earthly satisfied,
it clings to those it chooses
like a fragrance the youths attribute to
their forms. And seek the nameless,
though they have failed, in all things named.

And cannot speak of it who know not
what it is, weep to be understood,
are gentle-limbed and always lonely,
fall into bad ways and disrepute,
and cannot grasp that what must die
so they may rise are those named things
through which the nameless cannot be
achieved. And have not learned to kneel,
and are not fit for this heroic deed.

SA RIERA

There are some rocks out in this bay
rising like pyramids above a flat terrain,
except that here the surface at their base—
unless driven otherwise—yields before man,
gently to swimmers and to man-made craft,
unlike the characteristics of sand,
often impenetrable as theft, and wont
to cast itself into a lost man's face.

The rock is no architectural feat
assuaging a king's bereavement,
or marking a despot's journey to the sun.
Nor the relic of a people startling
posterity with what they had done.
On a still evening when the waters
are soft and calm as a woman's hair,
when a man standing up in his boat

guides it without effort, leaving
evidence of himself in the water track
as in a woman's thoughts for days,
the rock, gray in a fading light,
is unmoved, being itself the base
around which waters leap like flames,
or fish for food, and like a watchdog lies
supreme and deadly lest someone cross
the boundary guarded like sacred ground.

The hardened residue of bone, of wind,
of unanticipated turn and ages of events,
tears on the face of a sea, the rocks
in this and other bays have taken in
more human things than any mind
could hold. And what mind could guess
the endurance that stirs in them
whom death flies by like the scavenger
seabirds that pay them little heed?

ENCOUNTER AT TEHUIXTLA*

He was a farmhand, a youth
bringing freshness, innocence
to his beginning adult years,
coyly as a newly planted tree
in its first spring. Or so
it seemed to the two Europeans—
one still young enough to be
his older friend, the other
old enough to be his mother—
who had spotted him
among a truckload of laborers
come for a quick swim.

He was equally drawn to them,
would not take his eyes off them
as if he were watching a film.
"City people must excite him,"
reasoned the Europeans, "particularly
if foreign and he feels
he is in turn exciting them."
Which he was, whom they
had hoped to come across
in their flights around the world.
The Europeans had long ago
envisioned him, young,

primitive and handsome,
coming out of the sea,

* A sulphur spring in Mexico.

or at mountain resorts
in the rapid drift of early mist.
Now in Mexico, miles from
the nearest town, he stood
in front of them ready to bathe,
his farmhand's clothes dropped
where he was, his body fixed
on them. "His gaze," one of
the two said in French,
"could not be more charming."

"Like that of a slender deer,"
the other replied, "an animal
hiding behind a tree
looking out upon the field
with eyes trusting but wary,
dark and shaped like chestnuts."
"Yes, but don't you see in him as well
the fire of a rose
seeking to outdo itself in all its beauty
and be possessed
before this quickest spell
of total flowering goes?"

And mixed with that, both agreed
they saw him also as a girl,
a gentle creature in
a simple dress at church,
or at a crossroad on her knees
before her saint, or at her
lover's bed offering flowers
of the field, cornflowers perhaps,
and without uttering a sound
making it quite clear

it was body and heart
that she had brought.

But as the slender Mexican
who was indeed built like
a tender god, to impress
the foreigners threw himself
into the sulphur pool
and let himself be drawn
into the seething spring,
water pulling into its
whirlpool nest all manner
of things that came along,
whether they could take
the crashing force or not,

and as the Europeans saw him
fight this element with ease
as though in his upraised fist
he held an invisible spear,
he might have been a figure
out of some myth riding the water
as if it were a beast.
And what he showed them was this:
that he was a spirit in the flesh,
eager to jest with the yield
and turmoil of the earth.
Seeing him thus, the world travelers

revised their impression of him.
Handsome he was, and primitive
and young, but also strong
not frail and vague like some wreathed
youth risen out of the past.
When they drove off as if

to flee their thoughts, they did
not find him by the road
looking at them as they had
envisioned him, his sad eyes
saying many unsaid things.
Instead, for a distance out
they heard the laughter of the men
he had come with for the swim.

PAST DUSK

Going home last evening, I fell asleep on the bus.
The sky past dusk, lit shops, the many faces
passing by the bus, I took them in with me:
all movement that combined to form a world
      all merged in a deep sea.

They were transformed in me, the shapes I held.
Faces and evening lights flowed on in a new disguise:
lanterns on an unknown river bank, echoes, scents
      from patches wet and white, streamed across
the dream: I knew no sense of time or loss.

I gave them out when I returned. The stream
where I had been flowed on to a different sea.
I brought them back when I returned: the sky,
the evening light and faces of the world
      that I took in with me.

THE MIST FROM TREE TO TREE

They seemed this morning on their way to work
not mindful of the fog they could not see,
not mindful of an eye hidden somewhere,
the sign on someone rushing by:
the mist from tree to tree.

They hurried on.
They reached their destination one by one.
The eye looked on when they went in, when they
came out. Heading homeward on a darkening road,
a fog closed in: someone was lifted, carried.

REQUIEM

Winter's death fury
is clinging on to trees.
The howls on a bleak Friday
of a wind driving
some broken branches
and a last few winter leaves
down cracked roads; the sounds
like a wind's rattle in a
deserted house: this
the season's final agony.

A cold dampness and
a smell of wood exposed
to too much changing of
the elements is all around.

The tracks of a truck
driven when the road was
wet with snow,
have hardened into
deep strands of ground
disordered as
a woman wailing over
some terrible loss
in a terrible wind.

A waterbird crazed by
the wind's irrationalities
and the lack in the air

of bird-sounds that ought to be
abundant by this time,
lies washed up by
the agitation in the lake,
half dead among
the branches on the shore.

Go, body, go into
the holocaust. The spirits
that hang about the slabs
and crosses on the hill
may add to the high charge
and mystery of
the season's agony in death,
they offer no assurance
of a coming calm, a brighter hill,
and never will.

Go, body, go into
the storm. Accept
precautions you can take.
Fight each violent sign,
each new attack
with right submissiveness.
Impose no order
where order does not
belong. From elsewhere
there may or may not come
the strains of requiem
or other outbursts from
unworldly mouths into
a gloria or other songs
that clear all doubts away.

Meanwhile you cannot stay
and not accept the storm.
You cannot know the reason
for this apparent lack of rule.

Gloria
Gloria in excelsis Deo

(Yaddo, Saratoga Springs, N.Y.)

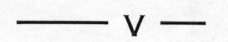

GENTLE LAMB

At a street corner
waiting to cross: two boys.
Pressed against the chest of one
a dog slender as a greyhound,
timid as a lamb.

Traffic is heavy,
the boys are waiting for
a path to form.
Here in midtown New York
on a gray winter day,

they are a vision dimmed
in most, are the dream
flowing through their eyes and skin—
fire on this frost-
and world-encrusted ground.

And like a flare
sustained and surrounded by air,
the dog enfolded by
the boy's arm
rests on a tenderness

the boy is himself
seeking to express,
a tenderness before which he—
also at home in

an invisible mantle
that clings to him,

gentle as a lamb—
is himself dumb
as the animal
he carries in his arm.

AFTERTHOUGHT

On your way home you stopped to shop,
looked around as you were going in
and recognized yourself in me
some steps away. Then you went in
and I went on. Of course the outcome
could have been otherwise, but not
what had already taken place.
That we had seen each other in
each other's face without disguise,
had beheld what is not yours nor mine:
a nameless recognition we might not
have reached, had our shyness and
each other's namelessness been breached.

MORE ON THE THEME OF
THE STRANGER

If he who is truly spirited—
not of this earth but on it—
were to traverse this street,
in his eyes views of the land
as close and distant now
as in former times,

even the stones of the street
would find in that land—
whose clear and always present
air vibrates through him
when he appears—
the perfect planes and lines
to which all stones are heirs.

INNKEEPER'S WIFE
TO ITINERANT STRANGER

I gave you bed,
I offered board.
You took the first,
refused my food.
"Thirst's a cry," you'd said,
"not to be stilled
by wheat or fowl."
Distance in eye,
you stayed to rest
but refused the best
from hand and tray.

SAID IN CONFIDENCE

Sense, sense
what my being says
and words cannot convey.
With eyes I hand
you innocence.
Believe, believe
in what I cannot say.
Though day by day
I grow more confident
parting the dark,
I cannot point the way.

TODAY'S TROUBADOURS

Troubadours in modern dress
lack lustre of the hearth.
In absence of fortified tower,
glow in window toward which
young hearts aspire,
in lieu of idealized love
what are singers singing of?

The shadow of themselves
on horseback in twos,
ramshackle walls in view.
The feel of their loneliness
expressed by untamed land
and lonely, lawless place.
Immersed thus with themselves,

with their restlessness,
their stance is not romance
but awkwardness. Gone from them
for a time at least, the song of praise
that gave many a troubadour
distinction for his lines
and splendor to his face.

CONCERTO FOR DIVERSE INSTRUMENTS

1

Vivaldi on the air

Trumpets in the background

Mandolins strummed in
a pace for children marching

2

On a bridge, one of many
crossing the Canal,
an eighteenth-century
pair of lovers lean

a spray of blossoms in
the upper right-hand
corner of the scene

3

Two birds fly by

Blares of trumpets
chasing them

4

Now trumpets mix
with mandolins

boat after boat float
under the bridge,

two lovers and
a gondolier in each

5

It goes on and on like that

there is this joy in it

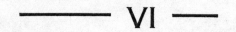

A HIGH ESTATE

1

Coming out of a depth referred to as
deep sleep, shades of leaves on glass
and shapes of trees
like lean bodies in a dance
mingle on my lids with
unrecollected histories
still hanging there. Sometimes it is
a bird's bright cry or mist
containing spots of light—
a mood of lingering dreams,
forms of a high estate—
that takes the morning body back
into itself.

2

A barking blackbird sails
across the sky leaving a trace
of fire in its trail. Grace-
ful forms of birches in
a patch, too early for leaves—
the trees' bodies stems for silver arms,
their twigs like artificial claws
oriental dancers put on hands—
quaver and shimmer
as though all of the air
were a mirror.

3

For weeks the small lakes
I circle on my walks
have been frozen. For some time
I've heard a rumbling underneath,
the ice below a narrow bridge
giving way gradually
to a small but powerful
waterfall. This morning
the grounds swarmed with birds
resting on their migrations North
and others who come to stay
when winter goes. Also this morning
not all of each lake was covered with ice;
on a good part a thin green
surface had formed like a skin
of water before birth.

4

First signs of spring,
a first rush of everything downward,
streams of air like films of light
over stones, and the body a target for arrows,
fast instants of everything changing.
There is a tree by the lake
bending and straining over it
as if the end of a tree's movement
were to recollect in the watery stillness
every one of its ancient moments.

5

End is absorption
akin to the knowledge
when all of the body sleeps.

6

The child is at times possessed by
moments that have left all time
behind them. How else to account for it
that in later years they break in
when the worst of departures
are no longer noticed? And a memory
appears like a sign before one,
and it happens that the sight of a bridge
whose entrance is guarded
by statues with wings, and the shadows
these make on the banks of a river
tamed for the city like a pond
in a private street,
are once more in the face of the man
become the child again.

7

The calm look, that countenance
upon which the world sees itself
as substance sees itself in eyes
through which it radiates, hears itself
in voices of those astonished to find
something golden has flown from lips
they do not remember to have parted—
that instant of penetration,
that first sign is said to be
a mere glimmer across objects
when least expected,
like some incredible face
dimly aglow in the darkness.

8

There have been other signs.
Of a heavenly infant descending in dreams
and taking up courtly abode
directly across my window.
Or in paintings of Renaissance artists:
two figures approaching
clothed in the heavy mantle of wisdom,
everything around them—
the bridge, the dogs,
the slopes and trees in the distance—
in nothing but the purest perspective,
the sky in their faces, the hand of one
lifted, forefinger pointed,
every gesture conveying an air, an intention
as though it were nothing less
than the highest recognition,
their ultimate purpose
toward which they were walking.

9

Coming out of a sleep of lands,
a sleep of narrow straits through which
great sails passed in utter ease,
a sleep of ages that cannot relate
to time—in one I had crowned
a brother king—was it a morning
permanent as an artist's cast
that I came out upon
or another dream of lands
when the sky appeared as

an immense sail or holy being's shirt,
all of the fabric a thin but bloody red
as though behind it earth and heaven met
in perpetual sacrifice?

10

The certitude in someone's eyes
or in a hand so knowledge-full
it must have broken out of dreams,
the depth referred to as deep sleep
and the depth behind the transcendence of
a country scene from seasons to
an eloquence no speech can match,
no mind contain: these the signs
in every substance shimmering of that
which in each thing is the same,
is in and out of dreams the same.

11

Because it is that which underlies
all variance, is that on which
outgoing signs return—
the dark behind each flash—

therefore and
because of that

here out in the scenes
that reflect upon one's face,
here out in the world
where differences interact—

O constant constant sacrifice

in the attempt to bring to life
the flame, the thrust, the breath
that is achieved and free:

the constant gesture toward
identity

here on the page
or in a stone
or by whatever means.

(Yaddo, March-April, 1961)

VII

TO A YOUNG POET

1

When we met after I had read
your poems, I could scarcely help
see myself in you at your age.
Those eyes all openness
trusting without restraint,
asking not so much to receive
as to give and behold again
old memories they reflect.
Lips meant for creatures of
the gods, no one less, your body

designed for their embrace, so strong
a lightness floods it. No wonder you
could glide through streets
were you to release your wings.
You vibrate so with what you wish
to become, all of what you are
shimmers as though indeed you were
an illusion beautifully conceived,
a glimmering thing to make clear
to others what in truth they are.

2

Lest you think I mean to flatter,
let me say it is not you nor
myself I am speaking of. To whom

can the heroic stance in art,
the dismissal of earthly ways
be attributed? This has been said:
"Though eyes do not register it,
when the strings are played
and dancers have become the dance,
the gods are present then."

3

From what you write it's clear
your agony is love. You claim
you've been prepared to burn.
You've torn out of yourself
the best in you; you've offered
and have nothing left to give.
She whom you have named
your goddess for one night
vanishes; the hand of the friend
leaves emptiness in yours.

Here is no architecture adequate
for light and fire such as yours.
Your feet are on this earth
but who can measure the depth,
the extent of space and what
that space contains, which glimmer
in your eyes? Who but one favored by
the gods, what but what the gods
have touched, can reach you and
affirm the tremor that you are?

4

Because you see yourself in those you love
you are disappointed not to achieve
through them what you are capable of.
They have not wrested out of themselves
old memories of promenades where
masters and their students walk,
of sunset paths for pairs in love,
of streets decorated for statesmen
and their noble entourage. You feel
let down. Remember, poet, who you are!

The openness your eyes declare
is not characteristic of this world.
Each fluttering thing seeks a return.
All bodies fall to earth: this origin
the world feels in your eyes. Who but one
come down, around whose feet a stillness
spreads, from whose mouth nothing flows
that has not the flair of permanence;
who but one not of this world
can absorb its restlessness and pain?

Of streets, promenades and evening paths
as you remember them you must make
your friends, your loves, all those
you come in contact with aware.
For at least the time they find
a way to step inside the deep
perspective in your eyes,
draw aside your private thoughts,
disillusionments and all that tends
to make the scene unclear.

Then extend yourself until you have
become the vastness that is theirs.
Let all the music constantly in you
give proper tuning to your lines
and open wide the portals in your verse.
For the moment others recognize
the structure you reveal as theirs
you dare not fail them, awed by where
they are. This obligation is severe,
charged to make others aware of
the presence they are always near.

THE UNWORLDLINESS THAT HE CREATES

1

Alien in environments he has come to for the first time,
he is nevertheless at home in the eyes of those who look
upon the strangeness he creates,

is at home on streetcorners he chances on
where men stand about discussing events of which he knows
                                                    nothing,

is at home along the boulevards where the big hotels are,

in the parks at night when the crowds have left,

in the garden where on Sunday mornings there is music of
                                                    swans,
of peasant maidens lost to madness out of love,

is at home in these as a bird is above hillsides and towns
touched on for the first time.

2

As a face becomes real when contained in a surface that
                                                    reflects,
as the soul has an inkling of what it can be
when received in the eyes of a stranger,

what among the things that depend upon
reception by the heart
is comparable to the recognition that

the flutter of wild ducks, the cry
of wild ducks whose object of pursuit
the observer cannot trace—only the cry
pierces the park as if despair
had been sounded on a trumpet—

that such happenings one mild afternoon
in a garden of a major capital,

that the aloofness of a swan, its utter lack of agitation,

that these suggest the cold majesty, the grave
beauty of total self-concern?

That these cries, these calls, these cruel attitudes and
gestures,

that the young man lying in the grass his face resting in one
hand,

that the old woman sitting under a dark tree,

that both, and countless more
letting what goes on around them go by them as if
the cry of ducks, the target lost behind shadows,
the poise of the swan, and the anguish,
the reception in the stranger's heart

were no more than a slight wind touching the leaves,
no more than clouds drifting by,
no more than the mild shadow of clouds. . . .

To recognize these are no more than a slight wind touching
                                                    the leaves;

to recognize that to experience these,
to let them be like a final phrase—
name, place, days, years chiseled roughly in rough stone—

to let them be part of the heart's reception means

they have achieved themselves

and having achieved themselves have become less than formless

a thing for which there is no word
for it has not the shape of nothing

and received rest there as that,
as that without change. . . .

3

Who is he upon whom those who see him as a stranger look as
one looks upon someone who suggests a world at once foreign and
intimate, a world that though distant reveals something one
cannot quite visualize but has yearned for, has said its name and
responded with tenderness . . .

who is he upon whom those who take him as a stranger look and
are amazed, for he recognizes himself in the eyes of those he
does not know, who all at once and for a moment they cannot
explain or even remember, know him, and are astonished as
they have been when absorbed in the rarest of artworks, love
words, songs of dreams . . .

who is he in whom the things he looks upon achieve themselves?

He in whom their forms are released and become the essence that he is, and is theirs?

Who is he who stands before a painting in which the mother weeps, and the father weeps, and the son has suffered all there is to be suffered?

Who is he who stands before this painting, and weeps?

4

Whether he stands before a canvas whereon man's ultimate condition is expressed through the most gentle, most beautiful body possible,

whether he sits on a bench on a Sunday
and receives in his eyes the light
and in his arms the flesh of the candles
the women that pass him have lit
out of love for their husbands
devotion to their children and duty to parents
in the churches they have left,

and receives as well the songs they intended
the ones joined in
and the ones that shook their bodies
as they knelt or stood against a pillar
and the thought of a loved one who had come and gone
bolted through them,

and receives also the looks and songs of the men
on the day away from their routine involvement.

On the horizon the boats they will not cease to construct.

Out of the waves, out of the sky
eyes into which they can continue to look

eyes that will return to them what they had wanted to see

eyes that will make them what they had wanted to become

the look that will give them what they had or should have
                                                    had

the look that will wash away the darkness that had troubled
                                                    them

will lift them to their rightful place
and make them what they are.

They bow their heads,
in the evening pick up guitars for their songs of fate.

They weep over they know not what.
                            Except that
though it may be nameless, it is closer to them
than the wind of the sea on their faces
and the light of midnight on their hair.

And infinite the shapes, the forms of tenderness
their yearning takes

The expressed of the expression is always Love
Love itself hath said

and the shapes that rise in their hearts and are dimmed in
                                            their eyes

are all as gentle, as beautiful as that body of love
that died and dies for love . . .

And receives this, the possibilities inside them,
their mostly unexpressed intention, the quality
that pours from them as though their bodies were a watery
                                                    cloth
wrapped loosely around the quickest, brightest light,

as they stroll by him,
point a hand in his direction though they may be engaged in
conversation or may sit around a sidewalk table discussing events
of which he knows nothing

although at times they may look at him directly

and he is not there

only the look they seek,
the eyes they know,
the worship that is theirs:

the sign in the sky,
the sails they construct.

5

He in whom the pain in extremity is received and released

who is outside extremity or its pain could not be endured

he is not man, not woman,
he is not this, not that,
not I, not he, not you.

Movement transformed into art is an attempt to show this:

that form is so multifaceted it cannot be solid.
That color can only suggest color
and that color, movement and light
can only approximate
the quality the eye cannot behold,
the ear not catch,
the hand not endure.

And he who becomes he in the eyes of others,
who is alien regardless of the intimacy with which he receives
the streets he walks on for the first time,

he who is stranger to those who marvel at the foreign way
in which he moves—his ease as though gliding—

is it any wonder that when he comes into a street

when he sits on a bench or stands before a painting

when the sky trembles in his eyes,

that he weeps?
            For what is he but response?

And he flows into that which flows into him as a wave into
                                                    the sea
and the sea into waves

and both are water

both are one.

6

Festive the crowds the evening before a day of celebration in the
square that was once first in the city and is now famed for its
age, style, agreeable proportions, and the equestrian statue of a
king in its center.

Tomorrow they will go to the pools, will sing on the roads, will
lie on slopes, will eat on terraces overlooking gorges, rivers,
celebrated bridges, aqueducts, historic sites; in the evening will
follow suggestions of love through crowded streets and squares
with tall fountains whose faint spray the air carries.

They have draped flags around the balconies, there are candles
on all the tables of the restaurant fenced in by boxed hedges,
and many the languages among the people who dine; those who
are local stroll in groups under the arcades, and the places where
people eat and drink standing up are crowded.

Is it because it is nevertheless the time when separateness comes
into its own, distinct as a shadow in front or beside one, that he
turns from these, runs from waiters, from the sounds of food
being served, from drifts of conversations?

Is it because it is the time when those to whom streets and
squares and the names of the flowers that look odd in the night
along the coast are known in a language he cannot speak, are
strangers as he is, the night before a celebration, each alone in
the darkness?

In the taxi, back to the part of the city where the hotels are

and elsewhere and later
down the broad road that runs along the coast

he does not resist it, lets it possess him:

the demands of the night in a land that is alien—

and walks into the air to be near the fountains
and feels on his hands and face the spray that the air
                                                    carries

and elsewhere and later
takes into himself all that the light of the moon on a
                              restless sea is suggestive of . . .

7

When it is time to leave,
though he was alien where he has been,
and to those in whose language he cannot answer,
and to those who do not feel in him the possibilities in man
and the background he reflects, is alien still:

he knows that he has been at home.

In paintings, the folds of rich garments, the dove that hovered,
the movement of figures upward, spearlike, flamelike as a
                                                        prayer;

in the eyes of those who passed by him, sat near him,
who said much of themselves though not a word was said:

firm glimmers, kindling suggestions of what he knows best
rose to his demands and needs as waves to stormy wind.

As if on a stool near the chair of one through whom
birds roar, flowers sway, generations sing a tale—
from whom silence rises like a sword in flames—

attentive to murmurs that follow once the word was said
(what child has not experienced this?)

he knows he will be what those around him are

who will be what he is

and that they live not only in their songs and dreams
but also in the things they make—
things that retain their human presence like a hush—

and when he leaves
                              receives their looks
their flames in paintings
not as farewell
but beckoning, acknowledging wave . . .

and where he sat and walked

wherever there were those who looked upon the unworldliness
                                                       that he creates

all that is air remembers him.

                                        (Madrid, Lisbon, Cascais)

SHORT POEM

When eyes pass by trembling with presence,
hold on to the urge for possession of
the love without which you must learn
to remain content; then love with all you possess
that shadow wherein hovers a promise
like a young swallow in a thicket of trees.